Philippines

The Traveling Bucket List

101 Amazing Adventures

Alexa West

You've got a mission to complete.

A wild, unfamiliar, out of your comfort zone mission.
That mission?

To complete The Philippine's Traveling Bucket List.

With 101 Amazing Adventures, you'll get acquainted with Filipino culture, fill up on authentic cuisine, become part of local life, and truly understand what the Philippines and being Filipino is all about.

Not all of these adventures come with paved roads and crisp clean bed sheets, however. The best adventures are off the beaten path…and we'll tell you where to find them.

As you make your way through this mission, expect to…
- ✓ Discover the beauty of hidden waterfalls
- ✓ Explore lush jungles and secret beaches
- ✓ Climb volcanic mountains
- ✓ Eat strange delicacies
- ✓ And create sincere connections with local people and future friends.

This mission, however, comes with a price.

Upon completion, you will become **a changed person**. A person that is braver and wilder and who isn't afraid to realize that **if something scares you - then you should definitely do it.**

Are you up for the challenge?

Yes?
I knew you'd say yes.

To complete this challenge, you need only 3 things:

1. The willingness to break out of your comfort zone
2. The bravery to travel off the beaten path
3. A plane ticket to make it happen

And remember...
To live a life you've never lived, you've got to try the things you've never tried.

Shall we get started?
Here we go.

101 Amazing Adventures in the Philippines....

Table of Contents

Intro to the Philippines

7,107 islands.
There are 7,107 islands in the Philippines!

You could literally visit a new island every single day for the next 20 years of your life...

But the good news is...you don't need to. Not today anyways.

The key to exploring and discovering the Philippines is to know *which* islands have the most to offer and which off the beaten path destinations are worth the journey.

A country full of hospitality, Filipino people will welcome you everywhere you go. (Well, except for the militia in the south...but don't worry, we'll steer clear of that).

The official language of the Philippines is called 'Tagalog', a language with Spanish influence (thanks assholes). But you'll be happy to hear that English is widely spoken all across the Philippines, especially with the younger crowds. Get used to being greeted with "Ma'am" or "Sir" wherever you go.
It's the best.

Nestled in the Pacific Ocean, this South East Asian country has had its fair share of uninvited neighbors and guests.

Malays brought Islam to the South. The Spaniards occupied for over 3 Centuries, bringing Catholicism to the north. The Americans engaged in the Battle of Manila with the Spaniards, and set up military bases around the country.
Then WWII brought terror from the Japanese in the Batanes.

All of these crazy events have left behind a kaleidoscope of architecture, history, food, and religion- creating unexpected adventures everywhere you turn.

The Philippines is as diverse as it gets. You've got metropolitan cities with all of the amenities of the west, gorgeous white sand beaches with infinity pool resorts, and isolated farming villages that take 10 hours to reach by bus.
It's all yours to explore.

And The Traveling Bucket List is your key to seeing it all.

Here we go.

Chapter 1: Manila

Manila isn't just a fly over city! There's so much more to do here than just transfer from one plane to another... but most tourists don't know that. While everyone else in in a hurry to get to the islands, you'll be exploring the big city with less crowds, local prices and authentic Filipino food.

Photo by Paul David /Flickr

Between the sky rise buildings, traffic jams, and office worker watering holes, there is an abundance of fascinating cultural gems and thrilling outdoor excursions to be discovered. You'll just need a heads up on where to start looking...

Manila Metropolitan is divided into 4 districts that include 16 cities. You've got areas such a Quezon that serves as the financial district to more relaxed areas like Makati where you'll find lots of entertainment- all of which are easily accessible from central Manila.

Are you ready to conquer this concrete jungle? Let's do it.

1. Take a Filipino Cooking Class

The best souvenir ever? Cooking skills that will stick with you have the pleasure to accompany a Filipino chef to the morning market. There, you'll collect fresh ingredients from local vendors and bring back to the kitchen.

You'll learn to cook appetizers, main dishes, and dessert with techniques and recipes that are indigenous to the country. The best part of the cooking class, of course, is when you get to eat.

Most of these classes throw in a couple free beers or soft drinks with your lunch as well.

There are tons of cooking classes offered all over the country. Find one that suits you best.

Price: Starting at $30 per person

2. Learn Tagalog

A question you'll be asked often while traveling the Philippines: "Can you speak Tagalog?" Your answer? "Konti kang" or "a little bit" in English. Jaws will drop!

When you know even just a little of the local language, prices suddenly get cheaper, smiles get bigger, and the invitations to sit and eat or drink become oh-so abundant!

Here are some phrases to get you started:
- ✓ **"Magkano?"** translates to "How much?"
- ✓ **"Gusto ko"** is "I want"
- ✓ **"Oo"** as "yes"
- ✓ **"Hindi"** for "no"
- ✓ and lastly if you'd like to compliment a food made by anyone for you, it is **"Masarap"** or simply, **"Sarap!"**

If you plan on traveling the Philippines for a few weeks or month, meet a local for a language exchange over coffee or take an official class from Learn Tagalog Fast in Makati!

Contact: LearnTagalogFast.com

3. Filipino Cover Bands

Filipinos have such magical vocal chords and supernatural musical skills that if you closed your eyes, you'd actually think that you were at an ACDC concert or a live Bruno Mars show.

But hey, you'll want to keep those eye wide open because the stage presence of a Filipino cover band is just as enchanting. The lights, the stage, the talent! You can feel the passion from the performers on stage and the palpable energy from the crowd absolutely entranced.

Where: Monkeys Music Hall and Pub
Open: Monday-Saturday 4pm-3am

4. Salcedo Saturday Market

Photo by Cristeen Quezon /Flickr

Unlike many outdoor markets in the Philippines that sell common dishes like chicken on a stick or fried dough- you can actually find over 150 stalls selling gourmet food, artisan creations, and Filipino delicacies at Salcedo Saturday Market.

For artisan, try hand dipped juice popsicles or homemade jams. For gourmet, go with some cream cheese with garlic and oven baked crostini for dipping or lobster rolls. For delicacies, you can find pigeon stew and whole lechon. They've also got a decent selection of organic and vegan treats!

Prices are cheap and people watching is fabulous!

Open: Saturdays 7am-2pm

5. Ride in a Jeepney

Photo by Stefan Munder /Flickr

Jeepneys are the super badass public taxis that all Filipinos use to get around the city. They're cheap, they're convenient, and they're so fun!

Your Jeepney rides are going to be very social – don't be shy!

First, you need to know where you're going (roughly). While each Jeepney has a designated route with 'Makati' or 'Quezon' written on the front, don't hesitate to ask a local on the street or the driver of a Jeepney passing by if you're getting on the right one.

When you see your Jeepney, flag them down like a taxi and hop inside or hang off the back for an extra fun ride. Pay in the beginning by paying the driver or asking a fellow passenger about the price and they'll pass the cash to the driver for you.

To get off, ask a local again. They'll point out where you need to hop off. When you're ready, speak up and yell "Para po!" Once you see other passengers doing the same, you won't be shy.

How Much: 20¢ - $1

6. La Mesa Watershed

Even in the concrete jungle of Manilla, you're never too far from a nature and wildlife expedition!

The city limits of Caloocan border La Mesa Watershed- 2,659 hectares of protected wetlands and Manila's main source of water.

There are 50 miles of park paths within the watershed waiting to be explored; some of which are easily tackled wearing a pair of flip-flops or by renting a bicycle nearby.

On your watershed adventure, keep an eye out for exquisite tropical wildlife! La Mesa Watershed is a bird watcher's heaven with a vast collection of colorful birds, big birds, and even some endangered birds, that fill the entire forest with song.

Open: Daily 8am-5pm

7. La Loma Cemetery

Photo by Analia Gonzalez / Flickr

The oldest cemetery in Manila, La Loma is eerily gorgeous. Established in 1884 with 130 acres of sprawling land, the Filipinos couldn't have predicted how soon they would be at full capacity.

La Loma served as the resting grounds to thousands of Catholic Filipinos, many of whom perished during WWII when the Japanese advanced from the north in the 1945 Battle of Manila.

While most of the city was destroyed during the Battle of Manilla, La Loma Cemetery was one of the few areas that escaped its warpath and so, this site carries some of the oldest heritage and artifacts for native people in Caloocan.

Wander around the cemetery, respectfully reading the ancient tombstones belonging to people born in the early 1800s. It's spooky and fascinating at the same time.

8. Aliwan Fiesta

Photo by July Dominique /Flickr

Imagine a combination of Mardi Gras and a Hawaiian Luau's tropical drum beats....and that is Aliwan Festia

For almost two decades, Caloocan has been celebrating the Aliwan Fiesta where dance groups and performers travel from all over the island to participate in a day of extravagant parades and performances. The streets fill with Filipinos dressed in intricate costumes that take your breath away. Music fills the air as the performers beat handmade drums and shake beads like maracas. There is also a beauty pageant with girls wearing intricate dresses and stunning accessories. All to celebrate native Filipino culture and customs.

When: The day changes every year, but is typically help from late March-Early April

9. Wanderland Music Festival

Journey back in time to Woodstock (without all the boobies) where you're not live- streaming the entire show. Instead, you sink into the music and into the moment with boho chic vibes and a 70's feel.

Wanderland Music Festival is one of the biggest music festivals here in the Philippines with both local and international indie bands. Some big deal headliners have included Death Cab for Cutie, Lauv, Kodaline - you get the picture.

Like Burning Man has 'Burners', Wanderland Festival has 'wanderers'. These festival fans are a fair mix of foreigners and locals- all of whom come together to create a community that transcends beyond the music.

Open: Every year, March or April
How much : $93 (Regular ticket price)

Chapter 2: The Rest of Luzon Island

After you've had your fill of Manila, there's so much more to explore on Luzon island! You can find isolated farming villages, wild music festivals, and some of the most gorgeous mountain hikes in the country...if you're willing to do what it takes to get there.

Pagudpud

10. Banaue Rice Terraces

Photo by Jon Rawlinson /Flickr

Top 5 Bucket List Activity in the Philippines!

Many people consider the Banaue Rice Terraces to be the "Eighth Wonder of the World" and it is easy to see why. The terraces are 2,000 years old and they were carved into the mountains of Ifugao with primitive tools, creating a cascade of shimmering green stairs that mirror the sky like glass during the rainy season.

The terraces were created as a complex irrigation system for farmers. Naturally irrigated by the surrounding rainforests, the Banaue Rice Terraces are such a brilliant system that they are still used today by the locals who plant vegetables and rice for harvest.

Getting to the terraces is half the fun. No planes or trains here. After an 11 hour bus ride through isolated villages and rural farms, you'll reach the mountains where you'll hike to Batad Village. You'll traverse through unspoiled jungle, an amphitheater of greenery, and the mother of all waterfalls where you can take a dip in refreshing pools of water.

No need to plan much. Just show up to Batad Village and there will be homestays excited to welcome you for a night's sleep and some food.

How much : Manila to Banaue bus - $16 + $25 (Return way - Tricycle ride + Hot Spring Tour)

11.   All of the Beaches in Pagudpud

No, seriously. For some reason, all of the beaches in Pagudpud are simply referred to as "Pagudpud Beach". If you know which area you're looking for, however, someone will surely point you in the right direction.

There is the official "PagudPud Beach" which is a small local beach whose visitors are usually fishermen. It's a peaceful visit with some interesting people watching, but don't come here expecting postcard views.

Saud Beach is quite beautiful with white sand, turquoise water, and coconut trees stretching out towards the water. Half of the beach is private for resorts and the other half is municipal so expect to pay 20 pesos for beauty-preserving maintenance.

Maira-ira Beach might be the most beautiful as it encompasses a blue lagoon that seems to glow! Perfect for swimming and splashing about! To get there, take a tricycle until you reach the beaten path where you'll take a lazy, flip-flop friendly hike to paradise over wooden bridges and under hanging branches through the jungle.

12. Mt. Pinatubo

Photo by Ernan Tangalin /Flickr

Above all the other hiking spots on this Bucket List, Mt. Pinatubo is killer. No...literally. This mountain volcano has killed thousands of people, destroyed entire towns, and left sulfuric ash as a mark of its 1991 domination. But that was long ago.

Today, Mt. Pinatubo captivates visitors with its beauty, as if nothing ever happened. This hike offers some particularly unique features like Lake Canarem, Kalaw Forest & Falls, Sacobia River, and ash massage pools. It's like nature's theme park!

For a hassle-free excursion, sign up for a package tour that handlea all of your transportation and fees.

How much : Packaged tours - $20 - $57 (depends on how inclusive)

13. *Mt. Maynoba*

Photo by Leonel L /Flickr

Out of a fairytale storybook, Mt. Maynoba will take your breath away.

With 8 waterfalls, stunning scenery, and a blanket of clouds at the very top where mountain peeks poke through the mist, this is definitely a Bucket List worthy adventure.

This hike is a 'loop hike' where the 6-hour route has been mapped out for you. The trek is fairly easy and consists of constant elevation between a couple of exciting spelunking points with ropes built into the mountain.

The most enjoyable way to enjoy this 6-hour hike is with some good company. You can find Facebook like 'DIY Travel Philippines' to link up with some other hikers who might be interested to join you and split costs of travel.

When you've gathered your group, it's most convenient to rent a van and head to Tanay, Rizal where the starting point is located. From there, you're required to get hire a guide who will brief you safety tips and protocol! To prepare for the muddy paths and chilly temperatures at the peak, be sure to wear the proper clothes and shoes!

How much : Approximately $15.40 per person (excluding food

14. Hanging Coffins in Sagada

Photo by Rick McCharles /Flickr

The locals have a strange tradition in the town of Sagada where instead of burying their coffins in the ground, they attach them to the sides of cliffs where they remain on display forever. This tradition gives off an eerie vampire feel but the reasoning behind the tradition is actually quite sweet. It's believed that hanging the coffins on the cliffs, rather than burying them in the ground, is the way to get their loved ones closer to heaven.

After you witness this beautifully strange attraction for yourself, there's plenty of adventure to be had in Sagada. Off the beaten path, you can dive into nature with trekking in the forest, hiking to waterfalls, rappelling and spelunking down cliffs, exploring caves, and enjoying the scenery in this mountainous village. Sagada is an outdoor enthusiast's paradise.

15. La Paz Sand Dunes

Photo by gezelle rivera / Flickr

Want the slopes in the Philippines? There's no snow here...but 85 square kilometers of sand dunes are waiting for you in Laoag.

Jump in a dune buggy or a 4×4 sand cruiser and tear up and down the sandy hills for a thrilling ride. From the top, you can absorb some attractive views of the water and look out onto the diverse landscape with the sand dunes bleeding into grasslands like a painting.

Also at the dunes is the opportunity to learn how to sandboard. It's just like surfing or snowboarding but on sand. The teachers will give you a mini lesson and then set you on your own to play around.

16.   Ta'al Volcano and Lake

Photo by Jess C /Flickr

Ta'al Volcano and Lake are the pride and joy of Tagaytay City.

With 33 eruptions, it's the second most active volcano in the Philippines. Its signature is a huge cratered mouth with hilly sides that spill out into the Lake. But look a little bit closer and you'll see that within the cratered mouth is a whole other Lake. And within that Lake, is another island.

Did you follow that? There is a volcano on a Lake, which has a Lake inside the volcano that has an island inside that Lake. If you're still confused, that's understandable. You'll have to visit to see for yourself.

The hike itself can takes just around 1 hour and has a $1 entrance fee (what a bargain). And when you get to the top, you can hit golf balls into the volcano lake. Why? I don't know. But it's super fun and there are no wild life living in there so you can have some irresponsible fun without the environmental guilt.

17. Bolinao Falls 1 & 2

Photo by DM / Flickr

Insanely gorgeous! Bolinao Falls 1 is one of the only waterfalls in Luzon with a glowing turquoise pool of water! The falls jet down from 2-stories high into an expansive swimming pool below where you can play all day. There are varying depths to this large pool that will suit all swimming levels, including a partially submerged rock platform and even steps to climb into the pool.

Next is Bolinao Falls 2. Despite having come in second place with its name, Bolinao Falls 2 is number one in terms of pure beauty. This natural waterfall and swimming pool looks more like an outdoor waterpark than an act of nature.

The main waterfall is huge both in height and length. The pools are deep so go ahead and cliff dive from above! There are mini rock islands all throughout the pool where you can climb- some even have their own little waterfalls.

Better yet: neither of these falls require much of a trek to get there.

18. Summer Siren Festival

Imagine if the Fyre Festival wasn't a scam. You'd get something like this!

Dance by the beach in summer, under the moon and stars with festival goers who know how to party. Summer Siren Festival isn't fucking around.

This is the real deal with international DJs, professional stage, impressive sound system, dancing lazer lights and an adrenaline-fueled crowd. This is the real deal.

Like any quirky music festival, you'll get that boho crowd with fire spinners, yoga sessions, trippy outfits, and glamping all weekend long. There's even an inflatable island where you can drink, socialize, and make some new festival friends.

For this 3-day festival, you can book hotels nearby or immerse yourself in the experience by camping on site.

Zambales is 3 hours away from Manila and worth every second of travel.

Open: Every May
Location/Address: Subic / Zambales
How much : Bus tickets from MNL to Zambales (Average) – $6 + $20.41 - $51 (Ticket prices)

Chapter 3: The Batanes

Smallest in population and smallest in land area, the Batanes will transport you to a different world full of simple pleasures and raw nature. Situated in the northernmost region of the Philippines, the Batanes is comprised of 10 luscious islands with a total of 84. 56 square miles waiting to be explored.

.

Because of it's vulnerable location in the middle of the Luzon Strait, just 190-kilometers south of Taiwan, it's not surprising to learn that Batanes has experienced plenty of invasions, occupations, and interventions by the Spaniards, Japanese, and Americans.

 Luckily, these intrusions left the Batanes in tact. Today, nearly half of the land in the Batanes is made up of luscious green mountains and sprawling hills.

The beauty of Batanes is so overwhelming that it cannot truly be expressed in words. The beaches, lagoons, caves, and islands will leave you speechless. The culture here is just as exquisite, running at a much slower pace than the rest of the world. Villages, cafes, homestays...everything here is personal.

Prepare for an intimate vacation with the wind in your hair and meaningful interactions on the horizon.

Pro Tip: Batanes gets more rainfall than other areas of the country. The best times to visit are March - May.

19. Mt. Iraya

Mt. Iraya is the 1009-meter tall volcano that quietly sits in the town of Basco. Hikers and outdoor enthusiasts love Mt. Iraya as it's not a very challenging mountain to climb, rather it's a modest crawl through dense forests with crisp air with surreal views along the way.

When you get to the top of the mountain you'll find yourself inside the clouds which hug the rolling hills and turn the landscape into a dream-like world.

On your way up, you'll encounter roaming cows, hundred-year old trees, and the natural spring that many locals use for drinking water.

Rent a scooter for the day and explore dirt paths where at the base of the mountain where you'll encounter farmers busy in the fields and children who are very curious to meet you.

Ps. Don't be surprised if you are invited into someone's home for a meal. The people of the Batanes are extremely hospital and will be delighted to meet a stranger.

20. Nakabuang Beach

Nakubuang Beach is no stranger to international praise, including making CNN's list of best beaches to visit and the 'It' destination on my paradise-seeker's travel blogs. Why all the fuss? You just don't find pristine beaches like Nakabuang anymore.

Standing on the soft white sand with waves crashing onto your feet, you can look out from the shore and see Mt. Iraya in the distance and peninsulas on the horizon. This beach's trademark however is Chawa Cave; a curious rock formation that creates tall, mossy archways and shallow caves in the cliffs.

Unlike other popular tourist beaches that scramble to set up cheap food stands and hawk sugary drinks, Nakabuang Beach has stayed steady with the pace of Sabtang. You can find traditional cottages that serve up authentic Ivatan food seaside.

21. Tayid Lighthouse

Tayid Lighthouse looks like something off of a Dutch postcard. The tall, 6-story structure capped with rusty red roof next to a small cottage with a matching red roof sits on top of a brilliant green meadow with nothing but cobalt waters in the distance.

To reach Tayid Lighthouse, you'll embark on a pleasant 1.2-kilometer hike from the center of Basco. You'll be rewarded with a climb to the top of the lighthouse where you can look out onto the China Sea and the entire island of Batan.

22.   Stay at Fundacion Pacita Lodge

With no TVs and only the occasional WiFi signal, here is the perfect place to come and push the 'reset' button on life.

Fundacion Pacita Lodge sits atop an emerald pasture surrounded by rolling green hills overlooking the ocean. Every morning, you wake up surrounded by a vibrant landscape that makes you feel as if you're sitting on the edge of the Earth.

Each room has something special to offer its guests whether it's a corner view of blue waves rolling in the distance or a big balcony with a turquoise benches to sit, drink a cup of coffee, and watch the sun come up on the horizon.
There are plenty of adventures within walking distance, including The Honesty Coffee Shop and a boulder beach known as Valugan Bay. Plus, guests are treated to a free shuttle into Basco town to explore how these isolated people live their day to day.

How Much: $383 for 2 nights

Chapter 4: Boracay

Photo by Göran Ingman /Flickr

One of the most popular tourist destinations in the Visayas, 350 kilometers south of Manila, is the paradise island of Boracay. This island is a picturesque getaway for honeymooners, a bucket list destination for kite surfers, and dream come true for everyone in-between.

Only 7 kilometers long and 1 kilometer wide, it won't take long to explore the gorgeous 13 beaches here.

Fly into Kalibo Airport or Caticlan Airport on the island of Panay, and head on over to the ferry port to start your paradise adventure.

23. Ariel's Point

Conquer your fear of heights with a full day of cliff diving and water sports. You'll be whisked out onto the open waters in a longtail boat along with a dozen other thrill seeking backpackers and travelers. The boat will bring you to Ariel's Point where you'll climb up the rocky steps until you reach the main deck. That's where the fun begins.

You'll see that there are 3 planks from which you can dive, ranging from 3 meters to 15 meters. Start with a simple Pencil Dive or you might end up making a loud slapping sound when you hit the water.

If you want to play in the water but are too nervous to cliff dive, you can ascend the cliff via a bamboo ladder. There is snorkeling, kayaking, and paddle boarding to enjoy when you sign up for Ariel's day pass. This day pass includes a lunch buffet as well as an open bar to give you some courage.

Where: Everyday there are boats riding out to Ariel's Point from the beaches of Boracay.

24. White Beach

Boracay's main beach is called White Beach. The sand is powder soft, the water is crystal blue, and the coconuts are as big as your head.

White Beach is 4 kilometers long and is divided into 3 sections: Boat Station 1, Boat Station 2, and Boat Station 3. You'll find that hotels and restaurants use these boat stations as markers of reference.

Station 1 is known to be the high-end area; Station 2 is where most of the restaurants, bars, and shopping are located; and Station 3 is the quieter area away from nightlife. Take your pick. Order a drink. And chill out.

25. Haqqy Boracay Pub Crawl

#TurnStrangersIntoFriends

That's the motto of Boracay's Pub Crawl. Sign up for the Pub Crawl on your very first night on the island to start your trip off right with new friends and a lay of the land.

The Boracay Pub Crawl has been going strong for almost 10 years now and has no intention of slowing down. Join the crew by crawling to 5 bars, playing games and enjoying drinks at each stop. By the second bar, you're sure to have made some new friends...or maybe even more.

How Much: $13
When: Monday, Wednesday, Friday & Saturday @ 7:45pm
Contact: pubcrawl.ph

26. Mermaid Swimming Academy

Paulo Violas

A dream come true for both men and women! Transform into a real life mermaid (or merman) on the island of Boracay. Once you slip into your mermaid tail, you can use your sleek scales to smoothly glide through the water and your new fin to powerfully propel you to maximum depths of 10 meters!

Taught by certified mermaid instructors through the International Mermaid Swimming Instructors Association (that's a real thing, now), you'll learn how to move, pose, and swim like a mermaid. And of course, there will be lots of pictures taken for your Instagram.

Where: Fisheye Divers, Station 1 (next to Starbucks),
Contact: philippinemermaidswimmingacademy.com

27. Crystal Cove Island

Photo by Marlon E /Flickr

20 minutes from shore lays Crystal Cove Island- a small island with rocky cliff sides quirky art, and dilapidating bamboo structures that set the tone for a weird adventure.

There's a checklist of activities to do while you're on Crystal Cove:
- ✓ Sit in the creepy hand chairs
- ✓ Snorkel amongst the reefs
- ✓ Explore island caves with crystal formations
- ✓ Tunnel through the caves to reach the other side of the island

You won't need to spend more than an hour or so on Crystal Cove, so work it into your boat trip adventure!

28. Puka Shell Beach

Photo by dr_tr /Flickr

Also known as, Yapak Beach, Puka Shell Beach is located on the north of the island and offers something that the other popular beaches do not: privacy. Maybe it's because this beach doesn't have bright white sand or maybe it's because this beach doesn't offer enough food and drinks- but Puka Shell beach sees far less tourists than White Beach.

You won't find more than a couple guesthouses and cabanas for lounging on Puka Shell Beach. Play in the sand to discover shells and crabs, have a long walk, or take a quiet swim and enjoy the moment.

Chapter 5: Cebu

The energy, the people, the architecture, the food... the mangos. If Cebu isn't already in your travel plans, then you might want to make some adjustments.

As the center of trade, commerce, and tourism in the Philippines, you can only imagine that there is a lot to be seen and done in Cebu. From historic sites where Spanish settlers first landed to incredible underwater marine parks teeming with tropical sea life, you won't be able to get enough of this South East Asian hub.

Swim with Whale Sharks, visit some museums, and eat dinner by the sea. You get a little bit of everything in Cebu.

29. Canyoneering

Top 5 Bucket List Activity in the Philippines!

Canyoneering is a must. Maybe you haven't heard of it before, because there are few places in the world that offer this kind of topography. Thousands of years of rivers and erosion have created pathways, caves, waterfalls, and swimming pools through tall cliffs in Cebu- and you have the opportunity to explore them.

You'll jump off cliffs into cool pools of water, slide on your belly down naturally-made water slides, repell down steep walls- all with a guide who is a pro at making you feel like a modern-day Indiana Jones.

Canyoneering in Kawasan is best done with a reputable company called Kawasan Canyoneering (duh). They take you on a full tour, provide all your gear and snacks for one of the best days of your life (not even exaggerating)!

How much : $70/per person (
Contact: kawasancanyoneering.com.ph/

30. Dive with Whale Sharks

Top 5 Bucket List Activity in the Philippines!

The biggest fish in the world are right off the coast of the Philippines. Although they are called "sharks", these gentle beasts are far from what you may imagine.

Oslob Whale Sharks Tour Company is one of the most respected in the business. They guarantee, with 99% certainty, that you will witness and have the opportunity to swim alongside a mighty Whale Shark.

These particular Whale Sharks are considered wild, but instead of migrating to warmer waters for parts of the year, they stick around as the fishermen continue to feed them. That means this experience is available no matter what time of the year you visit.

How Much: $160
Contact: oslobwhalesharks.com

31. Dolphin Watching in Tanon Strait

The channel of water in between Cebu Island and Bacalod is home to some of the most playful ocean animals known to man!

Dolphins are most active in the morning and it will take you about an hour to reach them from Dumaguete. So, if you want to see them in action, you'll have to be willing to get up at the crack of dawn to head to the Tanon Strait.

You will be put whisked away on a catamaran boat with other animal-loving tourist anxious to see the amazing creatures.

And as you may know, dolphins hunt for fish in groups. They are very tactful and strategic in their tireless efforts to acquire a meal. You'll get to witness the madness as multiple dolphins swim, splash, and jump out of the water. If you're really lucky, a few dolphins get curious enough to come say 'hello' to the sightseers on the boat.

32. 1730 Jesuit House

Photo by Constantine Agustin /Flickr

You wouldn't expect such a memorable experience to begin in a hardware store, but it will. Stepping inside the 1730 Jesuit House feels like stepping 100 years back through history. Jesuit House is a local project that aims to preserve one of Cebu's historic sites. This ancient house has survived typhoons, earthquakes, and foreign invasions, yet still stands to tell the tale.

Your tour guide will take you through an hour-long journey while showing you restoration efforts, along with artifacts and antiques including cameras, carvings, furniture and even 100-year-old cedar chest that still gives off a beautiful aroma.

The newest project at 1730 Jesuit House? Excavating the property! You'll be able to check out what they've found so far including Chinese porcelain, clay pottery, ancient animal bones, and other artifacts... all hundreds of years old.

Open: Monday-Saturday 8:30am-5pm
How Much: $1

33. Basilica del Santo Nino

Photo by cb_agulto /Flickr

The oldest Catholic Church in the Philippines is located right here in Cebu!

"Mercy and Passion" are the tenets of Basilica del Santo Nino, founded in 1565, which still bring many locals here to worship on a daily basis. This Catholic Church holds a regular mass where families and children come to show their faith.

Have a walk though the church halls to see ancient paintings, gorgeous archways, stained glass windows, and overall, a piece of architecture that is awe-inspiring. You can view 17th century relics in the museum or visit the library filled with books covering modern subjects of all kinds.

34. Taboan Public Market

Whether you're in the mood to taste or just to look, you can find a wide array of dried fruits, seafood, meat, and nuts at Taboan Public Market. We're talking about piles of colorful mango, shrimp, pineapple and fish- a rainbow of goodies!

Everyday, locals come from all around the city to collect these ingredients for family recipes and casual snacks. As this is a local market, not many items will be tagged with a price. Keep your wits about you when bartering and haggling to be sure you get a fair deal.

Pro Tip: The earlier you go, the more exciting the experience.
Open: Daily 4am-8pm

35. Fort San Pedro

As you travel the Philippines, you'll notice a curious Spanish influence in the country's currency, food, architecture, and even their language. Visit the Fort of San Pedro and this mysterious element will become much more clear.

On April 7, 1521, the Spaniards arrived on the coast of the Philippines, which marked the beginning of Spanish colonization. However, Fort San Pedro was not built to mitigate the conflicts between native Filipinos and the Conquistadors, but rather was built in 1738 under the command of Miguel López de Legazpi to protect against Muslim raiders. However, during the Philippines Revolution, it was eventually over taken by Filipino revolutionaries.

When you visit this crumbling fortress you'll certainly be thinking, "Oh, if only walls could talk."

How Much: 50 cents
Open: Daily 8am-7pm

36.   Eat Lechon at Rico's Lechon

If you know anything about the Philippines, you'd know that lechon is a national dish that serves as the culinary pride and joy of this country.

In Spanish, "lechon" means, "suckling pig"- no surprise there. With the Spanish colonization, came this culinary gem, which is often roasted and eaten at large family gatherings and celebrations.

Lucky for you, however, you can get lechon any day of the week in Cebu when you visit Rico's Lechon. This will be the most succulent, juicy, flavorful pork that you've ever had in your life. Served with rice and Pinakurat vinegar, this is sure to be a dish you'll never forget.

Address: Multiple locations all around Cebu
Open: Daily 10am-10pm

Chapter 6: Mactan Island

Flying into Cebu International Airport will put you down on the ground in Mactan City. While many tourists book it out of the airport and head straight to the beaches of Cebu, the ones who slow down to look around Mactan are the real winners.

There are so many hidden gems on Mactan Island in the form of beaches, water activities, marine sanctuaries and more. Mactan is a coral island. Translation: Mactan is teeming with a thriving biodiversity that makes for some of the best diving and snorkeling adventures.

Better yet, these attractions tend to be less crowded and expensive due to the lack of competition on the island. While everyone is over on Cebu taking turns, Mactan Island can accommodate you in an instant.

37. Explore the Neighborhoods

One of the best things to do on Mactan is to take a tricycle to the southern city of Lapu Lapu (about 20 minutes from the airport) and just have a walk around the modest residential neighborhoods.

When you're on foot, you'll have a chance to wind around small roads where you'll find some of the best food. Many of these food stands are run out of the front of a family home where the cook has been making the same Sisig recipe for 30 years and is a true expert in flavor.

In these Lapu Lapu neighborhoods, you can also shop from the local convenient stores and contribute to the neighborhoods economy. Ask locals to point you in the direction of the shore where you'll find nice views and some spots for swimming.

38. Learn how to Free Dive

There is a school on Mactan that specializes specifically in Free Diving.

Freedive HQ is the best place to learn how to dive down into the ocean like a mermaid using no gear and no oxygen assistance. The professionals here teach you how to hold your breath to last for longer periods that you've ever thought possible.

The pairing of free diving experts and the amazing marine environment here will give you the opportunity to free dive with whale sharks, schools of colorful fish, and even Manta rays- with nothing but adrenaline to power your dive.

How Much: Courses start at $320 for a 2-day course

39. Swim with Sea Turtles & Sharks!

Fun & Sun Dive & Travel will give you the opportunity to swim with real life sharks! There are no Great Whites around, so don't freak out just yet. They will take you to spots where you can swim with White Tip Sharks and Thresher Sharks, just like you've seen on Shark Week. And if sharks are too intense, a sea turtles might be more your speed!

Also, Fun & Sun Dive & Travel has something called the "Underwater Scooter" which is exactly what it sounds like. You ride it like a scooter underwater while you're head is in a submarine-astronaut style helmet. It's worth a try just for the funny photos.

Chapter 7: Bohol

You go to Manilla for city life; Boracay for beach life; and Bohol...that's for jungle life. Expect a vacation filled with picturesque jungle adventures that will get your heart pounding and endorphins flowing!

As the 10th largest island in the Philippines, you can imagine that there is a lot of ground to cover! In the center of the island, you'll find the epicenter of nature fun with ziplining, waterfall climbing, cave exploring, and river cruising. South of the island you'll get your fix of white sand beaches and cocktails with tiki straws. You can also venture up to the northern end of the island to mingle with locals who aren't used to seeing tourists in their parts.

40. Chocolate Hills

Photo by Cédric Buffler /Flickr

The Chocolate Hills are by far the most popular tourist attraction on Bohol Island and once you see it, it's easy to understand why. Here lay hundreds of symmetrical green mountainous hills as far as the eye can see. You've never seen anything like it.

During the dry season, these hills take on a milk-chocolate color- hence "Chocolate Hills". During the rainy season, they are lush and green.

Hire a motorbike taxi to take you and enjoy the winding roads, stopping by sights along the way and taking in to gorgeous forests and scenery that surrounds you.

How Much: $1 entry fee

41.   Bamboo Hanging Bridge

Photo by shankar s. /Flickr

Visit the Bamboo Hanging Bridge where you'll walk across a bamboo-weaved bridge over the slow flowing river. Each step on the bridge gives you a little tingle up your back as it feels quite delicate- but not to worry as the bridge is suspended with sturdy cables that won't let you fall!

Once you cross the bridge, there are little souvenir shops to purchase magnets, bags, shirts, and more.

42. Take an Unofficial Cruise Down Loboc River

Top 5 Bucket List Activity in the Philippines!

Right down the road from the Bamboo Hanging Bridge, you'll drive along side a small river surrounded by virgin jungle, where locals have built a few tiny fishing huts and small vendor stations selling snacks. Some of these locals own small wooden boats and are happy to take you for a ride. You can ask your driver to pull over and arrange a deal on the spot.

You'll hope on the boat (with a captain that may or may not be 13 years old) where you can sit with your feel dangling over the edge as you are surrounded by pure green jungle. It sort of feels like a scene out of the book, "Where the Wild Things Are".

At the end of the river is a fresh-water waterfall. Hop in with your clothes if you'd like. You can splash around in the shallows or duck under the waterfall for a nice back massage.

43.   Tarsier Conservatory

Photo by Stefan Munder /Flickr

Tarsiers- locally known as 'mamag'- are an endangered species and would be close to extinction if it weren't for the efforts of the Tarsier Conservatory in Bohol and other Tarsier conversation centers like it.

Tarsiers are considered a "dependent" species meaning that they cannot thrive in the wild on their own. Every visit to the Tarsier Conservatory helps fund efforts and habitat to keep these cute little creatures alive.

When you visit the conservatory, you'll see several of these little frog-fingers primates hanging out in the trees, sleeping under leaves and staring at you with their great big eyes. The tour only lasts 20 minutes because they don't want to stress these Tarsiers out, but it's totally worth it.

44. Habitat Butterfly Conservation Center

Butterflies, spiders, centipedes, caterpillars, birds, and flowers- come witness a dense collection of natural beauty at the Bohol Habitat Conservation Conservatory.

Walk with a guide who will point out fauna indigenous to the island, persuade you to let bugs crawl on your arm, and take a few funny photos while you're at it. Afterwards, stop by the restaurant and ice cream shop near the entrance to try some all-natural ice cream!

As the tour doesn't take much time- maybe 30 minutes- it's a great idea to make this one of many stops that you do in the area.

45. The Secret Waterfall

Do you remember the movie 'The Beach' where locals kept an incredibly gorgeous piece of paradise a secret? Well, there is the waterfall equivalent to that on Bohol.

Top 5 Bucket List Activity in the Philippines!

A trek into the jungle will reveal the most beautiful natural waterfall and deep swimming hole that you have ever seen in your life. The water is a bright aquamarine color, the waterfall is at least 3 stories high and the pool is the perfect temperature for swimming. You can jump off a tall cliff, slide down smooth rocks and hang out with a couple locals who may be surprised to see you.

There are no tours going here, so you'll have to befriend a local and ask them to take you.

46.   Dimiao Twin Waterfalls

Despite being named the "twin" waterfalls, there are actually 3 waterfalls in the vicinity. Take a van to Dimiao public market where you can wander around looking at crafts and snacks. Outside the market, you can find plenty of drivers waiting to take tourists like you to the waterfalls- it's all standard business.

The tour guides will drive you, trek with you, take your pictures, while you splash around in the cool pool surrounded by nothing but nature. The waterfalls are breathtakingly beautiful with turquoise water to swim in, heavy waterfalls to lie under, rocks to climb on, cliffs to jump off, and rafts to play on.

Pro Tip: bring a picnic and invite your guide to join in.

When you're all tuckered out, your driver will take you back to the market where you can journey home.

47.　Cambuyo Rice Terraces

Rice terraces, with their sprawling flat plains and bright green colors, are a signature of Asia. In mucky plains of muddy water, farmers plant rice seeds that grow long green stems creating gorgeous landscapes. It isn't that rice needs water to grow, but rather, the water ensures that the rice do not become compromised with fungus or disease.

In the Philippines, rice represents a huge source of sustenance and commerce with thousands of Filipinos working in rice fields day to day. Hop out of your vehicle on the side of the road to take it all in and you'll surely see some farmers working

away. Feel free to snap a few photos of the rice plains, just be respectful of the farmers.

48.   Go Night Kayaking

Photo by Chris Lockwood /Flickr

Kayakasia Philippines offers a kayaking experience like you've never had before. Start your trip while the sun is out, paddling down the still river while looking upon the banks filled with wildlife. As the sun sets, the sky turns to beautiful shades of orange and pink. Then, when it starts to get dark, fireflies become active. The trees begin to glow a fluorescent green color and some fireflies dance in the air- all while you paddle alongside and under them. It truly is a magical experience.

Don't worry about your paddling level or kayaking competence, as KayakAsia Philippines will give you a short lesson before you enter the kayak.

Chapter 8: Panglao

Panglao is one of the only small islands in the Philippines that doesn't require a boat to get there! Just a quick drive over the bridge that connects it with the island of Bohol and you have arrived!

Panglao is the perfect island to spend a few days or even a week just living life in the slow lane. Spend one day hopping from one white sand beach to another or creating you own bar crawl, meeting locals and travelers.

When you feel a sudden burst of motivation to do something active, there are plenty idyllic spots for snorkeling, kayaking, and diving. This place is the total package.

49. Wander Alona Beach

Photo by Kullez /Flickr

Here is where the magic happens! Alona Beach is the main beach on Panglao. This is where you'll find the seaside restaurants with awesome views of the water, laidback beachfront bars where you can drink late into the night, and plenty of tour hawkers that want to take you on a trip into Bohol or on a boat around the island.

Alona Beach is home to some lovely guesthouses that stretch back into the jungle. You'll find cabanas with pebble walkways and tropical flowers, and you'll also find modest homestays for dirt cheap. It's the best of both worlds.

50. Get a Beach Massage

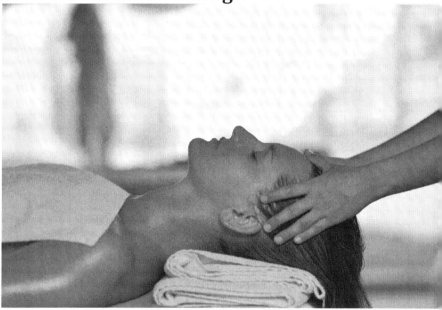

If you are not interested in a massage, it can be hard to shake the friendly and persistent massage ladies who have their massage beds set up under shady canopies on the beach. They practically form a human wall to get you to come in. It's quite impressive.

But if you *are* looking for a massage, then you're in luck! Lay on down and let these experienced masseuses work their magic. Prices are reasonable and the view is perfect.

The massage girls are there all day so you can just rock up when you're ready. Or if you'd prefer a massage at a later time, you can arrange house calls and have them come to your room- this is perfect for rainy days.

51. Go Scuba Diving

Right off the coast of Panglao are some dive sites sure to leave an imprint on your memory.

There is Balicasag Island where you'll come across dive-worthy topography including steep walls and deep slopes where rich reefs have developed.

Then there is Pamilacan Island where it is possible to see and swim with dolphins, whale sharks, and even Manta rays.

You'll find plenty of dive shops that are happy to take you out for some underwater adventures. Two of the most respected dive shops in the area are Bohol Divers Club and Alona Divers.

52. Snorkel Boat Trip

Sure, you can rent a snorkel and swim just off the shore of Panglao where you'll see a couple fish and some reefs, but if you really want a cool snorkel experience, then hire a boat to take you to the best destinations.

The captains of the boat will know the best snorkel spots to cruise to, including Pamilacan Island, home to a small reef island with lots of colorful fish. There is a chance for you to see dolphins, Manta rays, and whale sharks even without diving deep.

The guides provide the snorkels, but don't provide any sunscreen! Bring some with you!

53. Explore the Hinagdanan Cave

Photo by David Quitoriano /Flickr

Are you brave enough to swim in the deep dark waters of this bat cave? Don't worry, there are no scary creatures swimming around to pull you under. This cave might look extra creepy with spikes hanging from the ceiling and bats flying all around, but it's quite a fun experience.

The opening to Hinahdanan Cave is merely a small hole in the ground- you might miss it if you're not looking for it closely. To explore, you'll ascend into darkness via a sturdy set of stairs and the tour will begin.

A guide will walk you through the cave, telling you a bit about the origins of its formation. The cave is a little spooky with spike-like cave rocks hanging down by the thousands with bats flying all around the ceiling.

There is a cold pool at the base of the cave where you can swim, if you dare. Nearby is one basketball size hole in the cave's ceiling of the cave that shines down on you like an alien is about to beam you up. It makes for an epic photo opportunity.

Chapter 9: Siquijor Island

An island of witchcraft, healing, spiritual rituals, and…. beaches. Siquijor is truly a one of a kind island.

For centuries, the indigenous people on this tiny island off the coast of Bohol have been living in the mountains where they brew and concoct special potions to cure physical ailments, treat emotional scars, and to dispel evil spirits.

Unless you need an exorcism, however, you might be more interested to know what kind of adventures this island has in store for you. As with most islands in the Visayas, Siquijor is a vacationer's paradise with white sand beaches, turquoise water, mysterious caves, incredible reefs, sublime snorkel spots, and gorgeous guesthouses. With one of the highest literacy rates in the country, you can expect lots of friendly locals who are eager to speak English with you.

To get there, catch a ferryboat from Dumaguete or Tagbilaran that will take you to the Siquijor port where you'll be able to catch a tricycle into town.

54. Old Enchanted Balete Tree

As with many sites on Siquijor, the Balete Tree has a mystical and spiritual background. This 400-year old tree is often used for sacred rituals by the local shamen. It's unlikely that you will stumble upon any witchcraft during your visit, however.

Instead, you'll be dipping your toes into the fishpond at the base of the tree. Have a seat and let the fish eat the dead skin off you're the soles of your feet. While you sit, you can gawk at the size of this majestic Balete Tree with hundreds of thick vines hanging all around. Come to think of it, this tree does look like the best place for witchcraft.

55. Lugnason Falls

No visit to a Philippine island would be complete without a trip to a magnificent waterfall. Lugnason Falls is idyllic with clear rushing water that spills out into a turquoise basin below. The depth of the pool is perfect for swimming and the pressure from the falls is usually ideal for getting an aqua back massage.

The fall's water comes from a steam up above that is fed by a natural spring. For a few years, the spring was totally dried up and there were no falls. Then, it is said that local shaman blessed the springs and water came back to life.

56. Rent a Scooter

Siquijor is an imperfect circle with well paved roads , that make for a nostalgic day of a 'wind in your hair' scooter adventure.

Rent a motorbike and take your own tour of the easy-riding island. As you drive, you'll pass signs for popular tourists spots such as the butterfly sanctuary, waterfalls, caves, and beaches. Plan nothing, except to detour whenever you pass an exciting sign!

Best news of all: Siquijor is an extremely safe island in terms of crime, so don't be afraid to follow dirt paths or side streets and see where they lead. This is often the best way to find great restaurants, and contribute to local neighborhood convenience stores, and find unspoiled beauty off the beaten path.

Plus, the locals and their children are super friendly and will greet you with a smile or an invitation to play some games.

Chapter 10: Palawan

When most people think of Palawan, their minds automatically go to El Nido and Coron. However, there is so much more wildlife, island hopping, wreck diving and food devouring to be done on this island!

Don't be afraid to go off the beaten path and discover off the beaten path areas where the food is cheap, the beer is colder, and the beaches are a lot less crowded.

Detour into a mid-sized city like Roxas or Brooke's Point that are full of authentic Filipino food, quiet waterfalls, peaceful wildlife sanctuaries, and incredible local experiences. It's often the most unsuspecting areas that have the most unforgettable experience waiting. Find something on this list that speaks to you, pack your bag and just go!

57. Tabon Caves

At the very tip of a large peninsula jetting off the southern half of Palawan, you'll find the Tabon Caves. The Tabon Caves are significant for the Philippines as it is home to one the oldest discoveries of human inhabitants. Remains of the Tabon man, along with his artifacts, were found at this very site. Hence, the Tabon Caves are also a National Museum.

When you visit, there are 2 large, cathedral-type caves for you to explore, named the Diwata Cave and Liyang Cave. Hire a boat to take you over and point you in the right direction. When you find the caves, your jaw will drop. The limestone formations nestled into jungle brush look alien. As you walk through, there are small signs dishing out historical information to tie the whole experience together.

58. Underground River

At 8.2 kilometers of winding water, this is one of the longest underground rivers in the world! Officially labeled the '7th New Wonder of the Natural World', the underground river in Palawan is a must-do.

You'll take a short hike through the jungle where monkeys will come out and beg you for snacks, and then you'll reach small boats at the mouth of the cave. Climb in and you'll paddle together through complex cave tunnels with hanging bats and calm waters. You'll learn all about the formations from your friendly guide as you go.

Recognize that these tours are so popular that they can be full for a few days in advance. Plan your trip now by booking with a tour group online

59. Live Aboard Dive Trip

To see the most amazing dive site of your life, you'll have to spend a week living on a boat to get there; an experience in itself.

What makes Tubbataha Reef National Marine Park so unbelievable for diving is the fact that it's in the middle of no where. That means its out of the way of pollution, construction, and erosion caused by humans. The reefs and sea life here are all still beautifully in tact. In fact, Tubbataha Reef National Marine Park was only discovered by a group of divers in the 1970's.

In and around the reef, expect to see thriving populations of green sea turtles, manta rays, 11 species of shark, tons of colorful fish and more.

Contact: seadoors-liveaboard.com

60. Starfish Island

As if you couldn't guess by its name, Starfish Island is littered with groups of starfish doing what starfish do best. As you walk the shores and swim in the water, watch where you step! These colorful and diverse species of starfish are lounging all around you.

You'll see many of the bright orange starfish with black horns. These starfish are poisonous but not to humans. You'll also find the skinny royal blue starfish called the Blue Linckia, the brown and tan spotted starfish called the Pebbled Sea Star and hopefully, many more.

61. Visit Port Barton

Photo by Fabio Achilli / Flickr

Venture over to Port Barton, a sleepy fishing town on the North West coast of Palawan. Think of Port Barton as a less trendy, less crowded version of El Nido where you enjoy all of the same attractions for half the price.

Go kayaking on the sea, explore rocky cliff sides, get a good tan while laying on a sandy beach- you get the picture. See how locals live as they fish, take their buffalo on a walk, or head to school.

You can find plenty of budget accommodation here at the expense of electricity. That is, there isn't any. Most guesthouses in Port Barton run on generators that turn off at night. No fans and no ATMs, either.

Chapter 11: El Nido

Get ready to cross one of the most beautiful, unspoiled, astonishing, inspiring places in the world off your bucket list. El Nido is the ultimate Bucket List destination.

From budget to badass, you can find all sorts of accommodation here in the form of hostels, tree houses, glamping, and cozy resorts. El Nido is quite popular on the backpacker trail, which means that western food is readily available, parties are non-stop, and adventure tours are well-thought out. However, don't let that fool you into thinking that El Nido is overcrowded because it's not.

You see, El Nido isn't the easiest location to access, but those who push through are handsomely rewarded with some of the most gorgeous scenery on the planet. The coast is a maze of limestone cliffs, caves, lagoons, and secret beaches that you could stay and explore for weeks on end. Inland is full of waterfalls, hiking trails, and Filipino villages offering of authentic food you must try.

This, my friends, is the definition of paradise.

62.   Small Lagoon

The entrance to the Small Lagoon is just a narrow gap in-between two big rocks. It feels super secret, which is half the appeal! When you make it through via kayak or hired boat, throw on your snorkel and get in the water! There are delicate corals to be seen with tiny fish that blend in with the sand. Plus, the water is quite warm here!

The lagoon is so small that when you're alone with just your crew, you could swear that you are the only ones that know about it.

63. Big Lagoon

Photo by nennnn /Flickr

You can opt to rent a kayak or hire a boat to take you to the Big Lagoon. When the current isn't gliding you along, you'll navigate around towering walls of jagged rock that look like they're CGI imposed until you come into a little inlet with bright sea foam green water with a little beach ahead. The lagoon is magical.

The crystal water is almost glowing, bringing the entire backdrop to life. You can see Sea Urchins through the clear water, and little fish, too. All around you, the scenery is stunning with islands in the distance and winding rock towering over you.

64. Simizu island

There are many island hopping tours in El Nido, just make sure your trip includes a stop by Simizu Island! One of the most fun experiences is visiting Simizu Island where you can hop over the edge of the boat and get up-close and personal with tons of curious fish. The tour guides will give you fish food to feed them and before you know it, you'll be surrounded!

From the water, you'll get gorgeous views of the limestone cliffs that surround a small stretch of beach. Some think this island looks like a natural, tropical castle. From the water, you can swim ashore for some fantastic photo opps in a surreal surrounding.

65. Twin Beaches

Photo by KC ABBY /Flickr

Together, Nacpan Beach and Calitang Beach make up the ever-so-popular Twin Beaches which lie in the north of El Nido.

Nacpan Beach is a 4-kilometer stretch of golden sand and strong waves that create the most mesmerizing combination. The waves can get a little strong, so it's recommended only to swim near the volleyball courts where the water is calmer. You can visit the resto-bars on this beach that sells snacks and beer for a chilled out day.

Calitang Beach is right next to Nacpan Beach but is much smaller. In between the two beaches there is a viewpoint that you can climb up gaze down on the entire layout.

To get there, hire a tricycle or a motorbike. Even better, if you can find an ATV, go with that option. The roads are a bit muddy especially after it rains. The journey will take you around 45 minutes from El Nido town.

66. The Best Snorkeling Ever

The companies that organize the snorkel tours know just where you take you so that you see the most sea life possible. In fact, the snorkel tours are so popular that there are staple tours labeled A, B, C, and D.

Tour A takes you to the Small Lagoon, Big Lagoon, Secret Lagoon, Shimizu Island, and 7 Commando Beach.

Tour B goes to Snake Island, Pinagbuyutan Island, Cudugnon Cave, Entalula Beach and to a snorkeling site in the middle of the waters.

Tour C will venture to Helicopter Island, Star Beach, Secret Beach, Hidden Beach, and Mantinloc Shrine.

Tour D visits Ipil Beach, Pasandigan Beach, Cadlao Beach, Paradise Beach, Bukal Beach, and Natnat Beach.

Every tour is awesome- it's impossible not to have a good time. Every tour also includes the snorkel mast and lunch. Why not try them all?

67. Tour E (Inland Beaches and Waterfalls Tour)

The most popular tour you'll find being offered all around El Nido is the Tour E-Inland Beaches and Waterfalls Tour. This tour is typically for 2 people as the transport is via tricycle, but you could always get more tricycles!

The tour will take you to the Nagkalit-Kalit Waterfalls and Nacpan Beach. The fee includes a tour guide for the whole day, transportation, and the Eco Development Fees. This tour offers the best of both worlds on land.

Bring shoes for hiking to the waterfall, and swim gear for the beach!

68. Cathedral Caves

So subtle, you wouldn't even know that this cathedral within a cave was even here! It will take local guides to spot the narrow opening between jagged rocks and cliffs. You'll go through the opening and into a cathedral-like cave with tall ceilings that were meant for Adele tunes.

Within the cave, you'll come to a seemingly out-of-place Goonies-esque sand beach with a beam of sunlight shining through a small opening in the ceiling. There are lots of smooth ledges to climb and lots of photo opportunities to be taken.

69. El Nido Party Boat

Unlimited alcohol, carefree travelers, and world-class scenery all in one place- the El Nido Party Boat is a must-do. Climb on the 2-story vessel and set off on a booze-filled island hopping tour with likeminded travelers. You will cruise to 3 or 4 beaches in El Nido where you can jump off and play around. There will be a BBQ on board and snacks all day. Snorkel, dance, drink, swim, and make some new friends during the best boat trip ever.

Pick up is at 11am and the boat will return to shore around 6pm, just in time for sunset.

How Much: $50
Contact: ElNidoPartyBoat.com

70. Island Hop in Honda Bay

45-minutes from the capitol of Palawan, Honda bay offers an island hopping tour that will make all of your vacation dreams come true.

You'll explore Pandan Island, Cowrie Island, Luli Island, Starfish Island, and Verde Island where the famous Dos Palmas resort is located. All of these islands offer out-of-this-world white sand beaches with turquoise water so beautiful that that you might get a little emotional.

You can spend the whole day island hopping in Honda Bay where you'll have the opportunity to snorkel, explore the inland of the islands, and splash around in the water. These tours typically provide lunch and snacks for your trip.

71. 5 Day Island Get Away

Go where no other tourists go...except for the ones who jump aboard Tao Tour's 5 day adventure into the unknown.

Starting in El Nido and making it's way up to Coron, this social and surreal boat trip shows you the remote islands of Culion, isolated fishing villages, hidden nature sites, and wide open seas that are inaccessible to the common traveler.

You'll spend your days at sea, stopping off to snorkel and explore white sand beaches, and your nights "glamping" style grass huts nestled in friendly Filipino villages. Best part of all, food and drinks are included- just not the alcoholic kind. Beer & cocktails on board are $1.

And while the price of $500 for the week may sound steep, you'd pay that price (if not more) touring Coron and El Nido on your own. It's actually a steal once you break it down.

Contact: taophilippines.com

Chapter 12: Coron

Photo by Caryl Joan Estrosas /Flickr

Remember when we said that El Nido was the ultimate Bucket List destination? Okay, we lied. It's definitely Coron.

You can consider Coron to be a smaller, quieter, and just as pristine version of El Nido. Just like its neighbor, Coron has natural wonders that defy logic and reality. Swim through underwater mountains, visit hidden lagoons, snorkel over opulent reefs, lounge on baby powder sand beaches- the adventures never stop.

As the north of Palawan has only recently made it debut on the traveler radar, you can consider that everything north of Palawan, Coron included, is still relatively undiscovered. What used to be a sleepy fishing town, is slowly waking up to welcome tourists to come and visit. This means that the adventures on Coron are less crowded, less expensive, and less spoiled than almost every other island area you may have visited in South East Asia. Before the world catches on and Coron pops up on 'Top 10' lists all over the world, come have a taste of paradise.

72. Coron Bay

Coron Bay is where all the magic happens. This breathtaking maze of deep blue water winds around tall limestone cliffs that remind you of the movie 'Avatar'- it almost doesn't seem real.

There are multiple ship wrecks in the by that have encouraged the growth of natural reefs. These reefs and the wrecked ships make ideal dive and snorkel spots.

You can sign up for Island Tours that take you through Coron Bay stopping at secret inlets, taking you to the best swim spots, and visiting a viewpoint that gives you to full perspective of this pristine location.

73. Wreck Dive in Busuanga Island

It's easy to see what Busuanga Island has to over above ground. But the real spectacle is way below the surface.

In 1944, dozens of WWI Japanese ships were hit in an aerial attack, sinking their ships right off the coast of Busuanga Island. Here is where these massive ships found their final resting place, making for the most fascinatingly eerie wreck dives.

Plenty of dive shops offer these wreck dives where you can swim inside and around the ships, which are now covered in colorful reefs and eerie underwater moss. It's an adrenaline-pumping dive that is worth the hour or so boat ride to the site.

You can actually fly to or from Basuanga Island from Puerto Princesa to the Francisco B. Reyes Airport. If you don't want to spend a pretty penny, however, Travel2go Ferry Service will take you from Puerto Princessa to Basuanga Island comfortably.

74. Bulog Island

If you're ready to make all of your friends and family extremely jealous, then proceed to Bulog Island! The sand is perfectly powdery and white, the water is a beautiful ombre that fades from a clear crystal to a bright turquoise, and the scenery is what Instagram dreams are made of.

When the tide is low, a fresh sandbar appears where you can take those coveted jumping photos that make you look like your floating in the middle of the ocean.

The way the catamarans line up on the beach looks like something out of National Geographic.

Bulog Island is a must-see destination in Coron.

75. Hike Mt. Tapyas

Photo by Travis /Flickr

We've found it! The stairway to heaven! To reach the top of Mt. Tapyas, you'll climb up an ambitious set of stairs that stretches 210 meters into the clouds.

As you ascend, you'll pass plenty of fatigued travelers still with a smile on their face as each step gives you an even more gorgeous view of the island.

At the top of Mt. Tapyas is a huge Christian cross that someone has actually been determined enough carried up the mountain!

The final view gives you an unprecedented glimpse into small villages, Coron bay, and the layout of the islands that surround it. Totally worth the hike, just bring water!

76. Swim in Lake Kayangan

Photo by Travis /Flickr

That's enough swimming off the shore; now it's time to take your water adventures inland. Imagine Coron Bay if it was in the middle of the forest. That is exactly what to expect with Lake Kayangan.

Put on some comfy shoes and set off on the 15-minute hike up approximately 300 stairs. The hike takes a bit of effort but the lush forest scenery will certainly help make the journey more enjoyable.

The lake is gorgeous with a shore that you can wade into. From up high, it's easy to see where the lake suddenly drops off into a deeper swimming poo. With 70% freshwater and 30% salt water, this lake is believed to be inhabited by (nice) spiritual beings and thus, is a spot where locals perform spiritual rituals.

77. Maquinit Hot Springs

Can you handle super hot bath temperatures? Take the plunge into 39 to 40 degrees Celsius hot springs in Coron.

The trick is to submerge your whole body at once and don't move a muscle! After a minute or so, your body will start to adapt and you will begin to melt into the experience.

Visit the hot springs at night when the temperatures in the air start to drop. This makes for a more pleasant experience. Not only that, but Maquinit Hot Springs for sunset is a pretty spectacular experience that gives way to twinkling stars and a bright moon against the dark sky. It just cant be beat.

78. Swim in the Twin Lagoons

Also called the "hidden lagoons", the Twin Lagoons offer a one-of-a-kind experience. The lagoons are essentially two small lakes that have been created in the limestone cliffs and are fed by the turquoise ocean water.

When the tide is low, the surface of the water lays below a limestone archway, where you can swim through to the other lagoon. As you swim through the water, you'll pass through warm spots and cold spots that just add to the strangely wonderful experience.

79. Kingfisher Park

Photo by Corentin Foucaut /Flickr

You're going to do a lot of beach lounging and snorkeling in Coron, so why not switch it up for a day?

Kingfisher Park is a mangrove bird haven with tons of natural life to explore. There is vegetation and animal species that are specifically endemic to Palawan; in other words, you can only see them here!

There are a few activities you can take part in including The Mount Lunes Santo Trek and the Starry-starry night Tour. But the most popular activity at Kingfisher Park is to kayak around the mangroves to get a closer look at the wildlife both in the mangroves and under your boat.

Ask a local tour guide about all of the above and he'll sort you out.

Chapter 13: Davao

There is something in Davao city that you won't experience often in other areas of the Philippines- and that is a local experience. As Davao isn't the #1 rated tourist spot in the Philippines, you won't bump into as many resorts, western restaurants, or high-priced tours, but what you will get is real Filipino food, experiences, prices, and interactions.

Go to a museum and learn about the city's cultural heritage, walk down a market to taste dishes from family recipes, or walk through acres of wildlife sanctuaries to create lifelong memories.

If you start getting that craving for white sand, Davao is only a boat ride away from some of the most beautiful islands in the Philippines where you can enjoy spectacular beaches with plenty of water activities for a day or two.

80. 6am Zumba Class at People's Park

Photo by Bro. Jeffrey Pioquinto, SJ /Flickr

There's no feeling like dancing like a fool with hundreds of elderly Filipinas in a lush park at 6am. While these ladies have the choreography down...you will not. And that's half the fun.

These little old ladies will be delighted to have you join their class bright and early and will find so much humor in your dancing feet. Don't be surprised if afterwards, you are invited to sit and have a coffee or even...be invited to someone's house for dinner.

To cool down after your work out, sit on a park bench and feed the pigeons, exercise with a run around the colorfully paved paths, and stroll the 4 acres of sprawling tropical rainforest, ponds, waterfalls, shady trees, and even some wild eagles

81. Civet Coffee

Calling all coffee freaks! Here's a brew you've definitely never tried before.

It's called 'Civet Coffee'. A civet is a wild cat native to the Philippines who loves to eat sweet coffee cherries. After digesting the fruit, the civet poops out the coffee beans. Apparently, this organic process gives the beans a deep flavor that is out of this world delicious and has no bitter taste.

Try buying Civet Coffee in the United States and you'll pay a fortune for these beans. But come closer to the source here in the Philippines and you've got a bargain on your hands.

For the best Civet Coffee, head to the base of Mt. Apo where you'll find a shop where you can famously buy a cup of Civet Coffee or a bag to take home for cheap!

82. Apo Island

Fancy yourself a modern day Indiana Jones? Then I've got an adventure for you. Apo Island really is off the grid – for both travelers and local Filipinos.

And you know what that means? Virgin beaches, unspoiled nature, and thriving sea life. Not to mention that the marine sanctuary looks like a Pixar movie... and it's all yours to snorkel and explore.

Outside of the water, this little island is can be summed up as "local". I mean, so local that there is only one professional restaurant at the top of the (climbable) mountain offering stunning views of the whole island. Aside from that, plan to eat in extremely small family restaurants where food is served in a tiny hut or from the front of a mother's kitchen.

Drink beer with the locals, eat food you've never had before, and connect with mother nature. Apo Island is a once in a lifetime kind of experience.

83. Island Buenavista

Gather 10 of your favorite people and plan the most incredible overnight stay on your very own private island off the coast of Davao! Island Buenavista is a small, pristine island with white sand beaches, clear water, full staff, comfortable accommodation, delicious meals, and water activities, if you please.

For just PhP $2,000, your crew gets all of that to themselves! The island is yours, which means complete privacy and total security with no day trips from random tourists. This is your chance to live like a celebrity with a full staff doting on your every desire.

84. Mt Apo

Photo by Francis Gimenez /Flickr

How about an expedition to the highest peak in the Philippines? "King of Philippine Peaks", as it's called, Mount Apo is one of South East Asia's highest mountains with an elevation of 10,311 feet which is 3,144 meters above sea level.

During the moths of March, April, and October, experienced and ambitious climbers can climb the summit during a two-day hike organized by various tour groups around the area.

Climbers will be rewarded with a 500-meter wide crater lake created by volcanic activity, rubber plantations, a 150-meter tall waterfall called Tudaya Falls, along with chance encounters by wild boar and deer. If you get lucky during this hike, you might even get to sight the Philippine Eagle!

How much : $132 (Guides, Tent, Meals, Processing fees, Vans, Certificate, for 3 people)

Chapter 14: Legazpi City

Legazpi City calls itself "the city of fun and adventure" and for good reason.

This city is home to Mt. Mayon, a 20 million year old active volcano that offers both wild adventure and captivating history. While you're here, you have the chance to explore around the base of the volcano with ATV tours, hiking, photography, and more.

While capturing unbelievable views, you'll learn about its active history of eruptions that have wiped out entire populations and desecrated whole villages.

.

From adventure to history and shopping to eating, if Legazpi City isn't already on your list of places to visit in the Philippines, it absolutely will be after today.

85. Mayon Volcano National Park

As Mt. Mayon is an active volcano, you'll see a puff of smoke coming from its peak and a small cloud of smoke hanging just above it. It's so idyllic that it looks like a painting! The base of the mountain consists of flat plains, rice fields, creeks, and rivers, all waiting to be explored.

You'll find many ATV tour companies in Legazpi City but Your Brother Travel and Tours is the most popular! These friendly and experienced tour guides will take you on the ride of your life around Mt. Mayon and the gorgeous scenery below. Visit the ruins, ride along the river, check out some free flowing lava- it's really an unforgettable experience.

Fun Fact: Zac Efron went on an ATV tour with Your Brother Travel and Tours when he was last in Manila for a concert.

86. Albay Park and Wildlife

Albay Park and Wildlife has everything a family, couple, or even a solo traveler would need to have an unforgettable day.

With over 300 animals belonging to 75 different species, there is a lot to see here. You'll find the rare Philippine Hawk Eagle, iguanas, pythons, deer, pigs, crocodiles and a very interesting museum with embalmed animals like a two-headed baby Carabao and a Megamouth Shark.

Rent a bicycle and tour the park which offers shady trees that are perfect for when you need a rest. Take a small boat out on the lagoon, rent a cottage for a nap or overnight stay, or even go fishing on designated days.

Chapter 15: Off The Beaten Path

Hidden, secret, or isolated – these Bucket List destinations require you to take the road less traveled.

87. Caramoan Islands

Rumors were quick to spread about this group of islands once the American TV series- "Survivor" spoiled the secret.. The Caramoan Islands' became a household name once the reality TV series aired. Still, 25 years after filing - the islands are still part of every paradise seeker's Bucketlist.

While there are no castaways gracing these beaches lately, the islands are visited for their natural beauty filled with glittering waterfalls, mysterious caves, challenging mountains, virgin beaches and tiny neighboring islands.

Go camping, hiking, rock climbing, or count how many tiny islands you can visit in a week. Live a few days "survivor-style" and embrace the experience for yourself.

How much : 1-way bus ride from MNL and Boat trip to the island (Ave) - $25

88. Cagayan Valley Province

Do you want to get off the beaten path? Because Cagayan Valley is off the with unspoiled green landscapes, infinite rice paddies, mystical lush jungles and mysterious caves.

Spend a day hiking and trekking where you'll bump into farmers and water buffalo. Go exploring to find the 7-chamber

Callao Cave. And take a few days to visit a homestay where you can see how slowly Filipino life moves in the villages.

To get to Cagayan Province, you can take the bus from Manila. It will take 12 hours but it's the cheapest option! Your other option is to travel via plane to Tuguegarao – which can be a bit expensive if you're on a budget. Consider doing a combination of both - going by plane and coming back by bus – to get the full experience.

89. The Town of Adams

Visit the city of Laoag where you can climb waterfalls, surf on sand dunes, and then head into the forest where you'll hike to a remote farming village that rarely sees any guests from the west.

You'll first hike to the Maligligay Falls. After a splash around, you'll continue on to the Town of Adams. This sleepy little farm town is like that which you'd see only in movies. It's very isolated in the middle of the green forests and farming plains. There are only a few houses scattered around, but some of them are more than happy to operate as a homestay when guests come into town.

Get a glimpse into how another people live and operate day to day. Your homestay will cook traditional dishes and be delighted to show you around the town. Or you can visit the Tilapia farm where you can enjoy fresh fish dishes!

90. Tinago Falls

Photo by ernette jaganas /Flickr

It's the waterfall of your dreams! A majestic cascading waterfall pooling into a basin of turquoise water surrounded by lush green jungle and misty atmosphere from the nearby cascades- you've just found paradise. Ride the bamboo raft into the middle of the gigantic pool to sunbathe, get a back massage under the falls, and splash around to your heart's content!

There's only one catch: "Tinago Falls" translates into "Hidden Waterfall" which means that you'll have to embark on a little journey to find it.

Your thrilling adventure will involve a couple of jeep rides, a motorcycle ride and a short jungle trek. And to be honest, getting there is half the fun.

Make your way to Iligan City through Cagayan de Oro. Hop on a jeepney going to Ma. Cristina falls or Purakan. Get dropped off at the intersection at Purakan and rent a motorcycle to take you to Tinago Falls. A local will be happy to point you in the right direction.

91. White Water Rafting in Cagayan De Oro

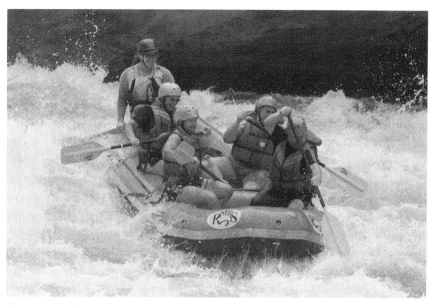

Photo by Bird Mom /Flickr

Cagayan De Oro, or CDO for short - is known as 'The City of Golden Friendship", although we like to think of it as The City of Adrenaline.

CDO is home to the most epic White Water Rafting river that offers rapids for every level from relaxing class 1-2 rapids to heart-pumping 3-4 class rapids.

There are plenty of adventure companies to choose from, most of which offer a White Water Rafting + Adventure Park Package where you can end your day with zip lines and water slides.

Great White Rafting is a very reputable company- check them out! They offer a 3-hour Rafting Tour that comes with meals, transportation and a day pass to the adventure park,

Contact: riverraftingcdo.com

92. Surfing on Siargao Island

Fotografías de Javier / Flickr

Remember the movie 'Blue Crush' where a mix of locals and foreigners settled on a small island and created their own surfing community. Same story over here on Siargoa Island.

Known to be the best spot for surfing in the Philippines, there's plenty of waves to match your level with 9 spots to surf for left handers, right handers, beginners, intermediates or advanced surfers.

When locals aren't surfing, they are enjoying the island with inland adventures like exploring caves, swimming in the Enchanted River, chasing waterfalls, or just renting a motorbike and touring the island.

Once you've worked up an appetite, enjoy the international community's wide array of restaurant options. From burgers joints to local Filipino food stands, Siargao has got it all. Plus...lots of small watering holes where the beer is cheap and ever flowing.

Pro Tip: The best condition the waves behave are during September to November

93. Tawi Tawi Island

How far would you go for paradise? Tawi-Tawi's location is quite surprising. This island is actually closer to Malaysia than it is the Philippines, which is why you've probably never heard of it. But I can guarantee you that after today you'll never forget it.

Because of its location, this island is full of totally unique culture and traditions- almost like it's own little country. Food is a blend of Malay and Filipino and the people speak with a unique accent. You've never experience any culture or community like this before.

While you're there, you can climb the mountain called Bud Bongao which locals believe can heal disease. You can visit some mosques, as there is quite a large Muslim population here. You can also visit Sama Dilaut Village where you'll find rows of wooden houses on stilts over water. Did I mention white sand beaches?

94. Swim with Jellyfish on Bucas Grande Island

Photo by Richard Schneider / Flickr

Swimming with jellyfish, exploring underground caves and tunnels, enjoying winding boat tours through mountainous passageways, and fishing with locals- that's what you can expect on a trip to Bucas Grande Island.

You've never experienced anything like swimming in clear water surrounded by jellyfish of all kinds. You'll find yellow baby jellyfish about the size of your palm, and bigger brown spotted jellyfish about the size of your forearm. It's such a fascinating phenomenon that you'll certainly want to bring your underwater camera. Oh, and don't worry- they' don't sting!

Chapter 16: The Foodie Bucket List

Let's be honest. Most of us travel just to eat.
And you're in luck as food is the epicenter of Filipino culture
and hospitality.

95. Jollibee

The most beloved fast-food chain in the entire country is Jollibee. Internationally recognized by world-renowned chefs like Anthony Bourdain, this place is not to be overlooked.

At a glance, you might think that some of their menu items are strange and that the combinations are unconventional- but just go with it. Fried chicken comes with a fried egg, rice and coffee; hotdogs are topped with cheese and they offer a spam sandwich with mayo.

If you're with a group, seriously check out their popular group meal sets that are just beyond gluttonous and such a novelty. You will get meals, for example, that come with 6 cheeseburgers, 6 peach mango rice plates, a bucket of fried chicken and more. Don't ask questions, just go with it.

Perhaps the most popular Jollibee treat, however, is the Halo Halo- a desert smorgasbord of red beans, cubes of jello, white coconut, shaved ice and flan. Ask almost any Filipino- they love this stuff.

Jollibee in the Philippines is like McDonalds in the US – they're on every corner!

96. Sisig

Sisig is beer's best friend. Anytime you see a group of Filipinos sitting around a table full of beers after work or on the weekend, there is bound to be a plate of Sisig amongst the madness.

Sisig is a savory mix of chopped roasted pork mixed with onions, ginger, garlic, chilies and fresh egg on top. It tastes like an American Thanksgiving stuffing or "dressing" but served sizzling hot – and often referred to as the 'Sizzling Sisig'.

The only catch? The part of the pig used to make dish comes from the head, ears and liver. It's not chewy or cartilagey. It's a really tender blend that, if you can get over the pig's head thing, might become your favorite Filipino dish.

However, if you're still struggling with the pig concept, try Fish Sisig. You can find this Sisig version at a classic food court stall called 'Sisig Hooray'. They're everywhere.

97. Isaw

The most common street food you'll find – Isaw. This Filipino favorite is essentially chicken or pig intestines on a stick. Yea yea, sounds a bit questionable but when paired with dipping sauces like Filipino sweet & sour sauce or gourmet vinegar – it's pretty damn tasty!

You'll typically find this meat treat grilling on portable barbecue carts or being sold at little roadside restaurants. Some posh restaurants, however, showcase gourmet Filipino cuisine and offer elevated versions of Isaw- a great starting point for picky yet adventurous eaters.

98. Philippine Adobo

If you only try one Filipino dish during your entire time spent on earth...it should be Adobo. A classic Filipino dish with Spanish origins, Filipinos can Adobo anything: shrimp, chicken, pork and even squid. Adobo actually just refers to the zesty sauce made of vinegar, soy sauce, pepper and herbs, which is used as a fabulous marinade.

The sauce is so full of flavor, that this dish is served very simply. Paired with plain rice so that you experience the full balance of salty, sweet and plain.

Filipinos love the flavor so much, that Adobo has evolved as a seasoning for everything snacky. As in.. ev-er-y-thing. Nuts, crackers, noodles, you name it and there's an Adobo variety. I dare you to try and get through your trip without trying something Adobo.

Pro Tip: If you happen to come across a food-court style restaurant called 'Adobo Connections', give it a try! Particularly, Adobong Gata for the win!

Open: 10am – 10pm (Weekdays only)
How much : Approximately $8 (for 2 people

99. Balut

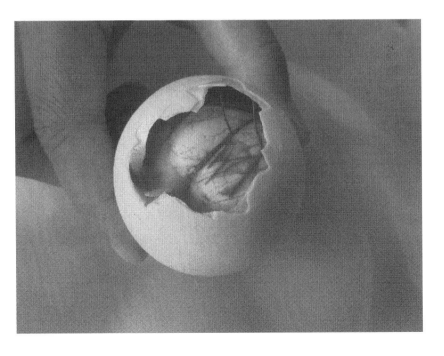

If you're ever heard about or seen Balut, it's probably been on a crazy game show with weird eating challenges like Survivor or The Amazing Race. That's because Balut is, well...weird.

At first glance, Balut looks like a harmless hard-boiled duck egg – but remember, looks can be deceiving.

Once you crack your egg open, you'll first drink the 'soup' from the shell, move on to the yolk, and finish off with the embryo. Yes, embryo. As in, a premature baby duck. Sometimes, the baby duck's beak, feathers, or eyes is even already developed. But hey, look on the bright side, Balut is rich in proteins and calcium! It's not all in vain!

During your time in the Philippines, you'll see that Balut is a very common street food/ daily snack all across the country. No matter where you go, there's always a Balut Guy on the street shouting "Balut, Balut" to get the attention of customers.

In Manila, however, the guys selling Balut are so popular that they don't have to should anymore. The customers know where to find him by now.

How much : 30¢ per piece

100. Salawaki

Photo by Mark Belokopytov / Flickr

With over 7,000 islands, it's no surprise that the Philippines is a fabulous place for seafood.

And Filipinos, having the culinary genius to turn any ingredient into a delicious treat, discovered the luscious taste of grilled sea urchins, aka Salawaki.

Never seen a sea urchin before? They are those spiky black things you see on the ocean floor while snorkeling. You can either eat them straight from the water or fry them up to brings out their rich flavors.

Don't worry; you won't be eating the spikes. What you're after is the roe inside. First, the sea urchin shell needs to be broken in half by dragging a knife down the middle all the way to the bottom- then it can be cracked open to reveal the soft, yummy roe. Eat fresh or grilled with vinegar or soy sauce.

How much : $1 per piece

101. Taho

You'll hear it in the mornings. Early. Think 6am-9am... the sweet call of the Taho guy.

"Taaahhhooooo". It's breakfast time, y'all.

Every city and small town has one. A man carrying a bamboo pole on his shoulders; two metal barrels on each end. When you approach him, he'll set his fast food breakfast operation on the ground and scoop out a fresh portion of Taho.

Taho is kinda of like tofu, soft and made from soy but with a sweet tapioca twist. Packed like pudding and served fresh from a little cup, this is the perfect compromise to start you day. You get a little bit of sweet and just the right amount of protein to feel energized enough to make it to lunch (or second breakfast).

How much : Less than $1

Mission Complete!

Or at least...Mission Started!

Realize that there are people on this Earth who live and die within the same 30 mile radius. There is an indent on the couch from where they plant themselves in front of a TV day after day and day.

That's not you.
That will *never* be you.
And the fact that you're holding The Traveling Bucket List in your hands proves it.

After 8 years of non-stop traveling the world solo, the most important lesson that I've learned is this:
Learn to trust the journey, even when it doesn't make sense.

Every little hiccup along the way, leads to something incredible – as long as you let it. Being invited to seek shelter in a stranger's house during a downpour. Getting a flat tire and hitching a ride in a truck full of chickens. Sitting next to a boy on a bus, who would turn out to be the love of your life.

That is what traveling is about. The destination is just what ties it all together.

So don't plan too much. Don't make an excel spreadsheet of your trip. Pick a place and just go. See what happens. Let life surprise you.

Just book your ticket and go.

22002318R00075

Made in the USA
San Bernardino, CA
07 January 2019